Scripture Confessions
for MOMS

HARRISON HOUSE
Tulsa, Oklahoma

All Scripture quotations are taken from the *King James Version* of the Bible.

10 09 08 07   10 9 8 7 6

Scripture Confessions for Moms
ISBN-13: 978-1-57794-652-6
ISBN-10: 1-57794-652-9
Copyright © 2005 by Word & Spirit Resources
P.O. Box 700311
Tulsa, Oklahoma 74170

Published by Harrison House, Inc.
P.O. Box 35035
Tulsa, Oklahoma 74153

CONTENTS

INTRODUCTION

This powerful little book is a unique compilation of Scriptures that will enable you to speak the Word over the situations you face on a daily basis as a busy mother. Whether at work or home, you can access *Scripture Confessions* and release your faith in God's promises regarding your family, and arm yourself with the Word of God for life's battles.

Becoming the Mother God Says I Am

I choose to glorify God in my role as a mother. I choose to live a godly life before my children. I am disciplined concerning my priorities as a mother. I manage my time in an effective and efficient manner. I am sensitive to the needs of my children. I have God's wisdom and discernment concerning how all my decisions affect their lives.

I am loving, caring, and compassionate toward my children. I keep my cool during times of stress and do not become frustrated and lose my temper. If I do something that is wrong or offensive, I am quick to repent and make things right. Because I live a spirit-controlled life, I am peaceful, consistent, and faithful. I walk in love at all times, and I am quick to provide encouragement and inspiration to my family. I refuse to criticize, condemn, or complain to or about my kids. I will be honest and truthful and live my life with integrity. When faced with the need to discipline my children, I will do so without anger. I will reference God's Word as their standard of conduct.

I will be steadfast and resolute regarding my convictions and will do my best to model the life of a godly mother before my kids. I will be faithful to pray for my children. With the help of the Holy Spirit I will do my best to mentor and instruct them in the truth and principles of God's Word.

Scriptures

...we should live soberly, righteously, and godly, in this present world.

Titus 2:12

If any of you lack wisdom, let him ask of God, that giveth to all men liberally, and upbraideth not; and it shall be given him.

James 1:5

...be thou an example of the believers, in word, in conversation, in charity, in spirit, in faith, in purity.

1 Timothy 4:12

Godly Household

My home is a place of refuge and peace. I believe that anyone who comes into my home will feel the presence of God. I choose to honor God in my home. I dedicate my home to the Lord; I consecrate it with prayer and praise.

I am diligent and committed to monitor and evaluate the kinds of books, videos, music, and movies that are allowed to be played in my home.

In my home are riches and honor; my God supplies all my family's needs. I will work diligently to keep my house clean and beautiful so that it is a constant blessing to all my family.

I believe my home is a safe haven, protected and kept safe by God's divine protection. I believe no evil shall come near my home, and no plague, disease, or calamity shall befall us. I believe my home is blessed and all who enter it are blessed.

My home is consecrated and dedicated to God. I will not allow activities in my home that are not honorable to God. With the Holy Spirit's help I will create and maintain an atmosphere of love, hope, and peace in my home. I believe everyone who comes to my home will sense His presence.

Scriptures

...as for me and my house, we will serve the Lord.

Joshua 24:15

And they shall teach my people the difference between the holy and profane, and cause them to discern between the unclean and the clean.

Ezekiel 44:23

And now abideth faith, hope, charity, these three; but the greatest of these is charity.

1 Corinthians 13:13

But my God shall supply all your need according to his riches in glory by Christ Jesus.

Philippians 4:19

There shall no evil befall thee, neither shall any plaque come nigh thy dwelling.

Psalm 91:10

The Greater One in My Children

God Himself makes His home in the hearts of my children. God in them is greater than any temptation, greater than any peer pressure, greater than any sin, greater than Satan and all the forces of darkness. God in my children is greater than any problem or obstacle they might face, greater than sickness or disease, greater than sin or any challenge that comes in their lives.

He is greater than any adversity they might face. He is greater than their doubts, insecurities, or uncertainties. He is greater than fear, worry, or anxiety.

The Spirit of God lives big in them. He helps them to succeed, He puts them over, and He causes them to be victorious in their everyday lives.

God's Word gives them boldness and courage to live godly lives before their family and friends. The same Spirit that raised Christ Jesus from the dead lives in my children. The Holy Spirit quickens and brings life, strength, and vitality to their bodies. My children are more than conquerors in Christ Jesus through the power of the Holy Spirit. My children shall face life with confidence and a resolute, tenacious faith in God, who always causes them to triumph in life. Greater is He that is in them, than he that is in the world.

Scriptures

Ye are of God, little children, and have overcome them: because greater is he that is in you, than he that is in the world.

1 John 4:4

These things I have spoken unto you, that in me ye might have peace. In the world ye shall have tribulation: but be of good cheer; I have overcome the world.

John 16:33

Nay, in all these things we are more than conquerors through him that loved us.

Romans 8:37

But if the Spirit of him that raised up Jesus from the dead dwell in you, he that raised up Christ from the dead shall also quicken your mortal bodies by his Spirit that dwelleth in you.

Romans 8:11

My Children's Spiritual Growth

I speak God's Word over my children. I proclaim and confess that my children are strong in faith. God's Word is working in their lives. They have pure hearts, and they conduct their lives with honesty, purity, and integrity. They love God's Word and desire to live honorable lives before Him.

Favor surrounds them like a shield. They are sensitive to the Holy Spirit, and they are quick to obey His voice. They are bold in their faith and want to share it with others.

My children are growing strong spiritually, mentally, and physically. They have wisdom functioning in every area of their lives. They put God's Word first and accept it as final authority in their lives. They are careful what influences they allow in their lives. The eyes of their understanding are opened to the truth of God's Word.

They have godly discernment concerning the type of people they develop relationships with. They are not easily fooled or deceived and have godly wisdom beyond their years.

They are individuals of character and principle. They are kind, loving, and giving towards others. They are not selfish or self-serving. They are quick to reach out to help others in need. They will develop into courageous, confident, and determined adults, ready to fulfill the plans that God has for them.

Scriptures

He restoreth my soul: he leadeth me in the paths of righteousness for his name's sake.

Psalm 23:3

But the Comforter, which is the Holy Ghost, whom the Father will send in my name, he shall teach you all things, and bring all things to your remembrance, whatsoever I have said unto you.

John 14:26

For I know the thoughts that I think toward you, saith the Lord, thoughts of peace, and not of evil, to give you an expected end.

Jeremiah 29:11

My Children Hear God's Voice

I proclaim that my children know God's voice and will not be deceived by the voice of the enemy. They are sensitive to the voice of the Holy Spirit and are quick to obey His instruction, direction, and guidance. They are tuned in to the Holy Spirit and quickly recognize His voice. They are mindful not to do anything that grieves the Holy Spirit. They are diligent to spend time in prayer, to fellowship, and to worship the Lord so that they continually keep themselves in proper spiritual condition to hear His voice.

My children will seek God's wisdom and counsel concerning all matters of their lives. I know He will be faithful to speak to them concerning changes or corrections they need to make. I believe they will be faithful to do everything God would have them to do. He speaks to my children through His Word. As they study and meditate on the Scriptures, God's life-giving force comes alive in their hearts. God's Word enlightens their spirits and illuminates their minds. I believe that my children's union with God grows stronger every day, as well as their ability to hear His voice clearly and accurately.

Scriptures

But this thing commanded I them, saying, Obey my voice, and I will be your God, and ye shall be my people: and walk ye in all the ways that I have commanded you, that it may be well unto you.

Jeremiah 7:23

And when he putteth forth his own sheep, he goeth before them, and the sheep follow him: for they know his voice. And a stranger will they not follow, but will flee from him: for they know not the voice of strangers.

John 10:4,5

My sheep hear my voice, and I know them, and they follow me.

John 10:27

So then faith cometh by hearing, and hearing by the word of God.

Romans 10:17

My Children Are Obedient to Authority

My children are obedient to me, and they are quick to respond to my requests. They honor me and respect me. They are kind and considerate and are quick to repent if they ever do anything to offend me.

Because they respect me, they do not ignore me when I speak to them but give me their undivided attention. They are not slothful in fulfilling their chores and household duties.

As my children honor me, then I will honor them and respect them. I will never belittle or talk to them in a condescending way. I will always be looking for opportunities to tell and show them how much I love them. God will bless and honor them because they honor those who are in authority over their lives.

They will not give in to the temptation to be prideful or rebellious. The truth of God's Word that has been planted in their hearts is the guiding light of their lives. They have God's nature in their hearts and a pleasant disposition.

Because they are obedient to me, they shall have blessed lives, and they shall live long and fruitful lives

Scriptures

Children, obey your parents in the Lord: for this is right. Honor thy father and mother; (which is the first commandment with promise;) That it may be well with thee, and thou mayest live long on the earth.

Ephesians 6:1-3

For kings, and for all that are in authority; that we may lead a quiet and peaceable life in all godliness and honesty.

1 Timothy 2:2

And the people said unto Joshua, The Lord our God will we serve, and his voice will we obey.

Joshua 24:24

If ye be willing and obedient, ye shall eat the good of the land.

Isaiah 1:19

Divine Protection for My Children

God's Word promises divine protection for the children of God. Therefore, I proclaim that no evil shall come near me or my family. No plague shall come near my kids; though a thousand may fall at their side and ten thousand at their right hand, it shall not, will not, cannot come near my children.

God's angels encamp around my kids. The angels of the Lord have charge over them to protect and keep them from danger, harm, and injury of any kind.

Though they walk through the fire they will not be burned. If they find themselves in flood waters, they will not overtake them. Though they walk through the valley of the shadow of death, they will fear no evil, for God is with them. No weapon formed against my children shall prosper.

God is their refuge and fortress. He will deliver them from the traps of the enemy, and He will deliver them from deadly diseases. Under God's wings they take refuge, and His truth is their shield and protection from all the dangers of this world. I plead the blood of Jesus over them, over any vehicle they ride in, over their school, and over any house or building they go into.

They shall not fall prey to the schemes and traps of Satan. They walk with wisdom and discernment and quickly heed God's voice. My children shall live long on the earth. They will fulfill the plans and purposes God has designed for them.

Scriptures

Let your conversation be without covetousness; and be content with such things as ye have: for he hath said, I will never leave thee, nor forsake thee.

Hebrews 13:5

Keep me as the apple of the eye, hide me under the shadow of thy wings.

Psalm 17:8

There shall no evil befall thee, neither shall any plague come nigh thy dwelling.

Psalm 91:10

And the peace of God, which passeth all understanding, shall keep your hearts and minds through Christ Jesus.

Philippians 4:7

Health and Healing
for My Children

I proclaim healing over my children. By Jesus' stripes they were healed. The healing, life-giving, disease-destroying power of God is working in their bodies. It drives out all manner of sickness and disease. They are full of life, health, strength, and vitality. They are healed, healthy, and whole from the tops of their heads to the soles of their feet. Every organ in their bodies operates and functions the way God created it, with no disease or malfunctions. Every system in their bodies operates and functions with supernatural efficiency. My children's nervous systems, their lymphatic systems, their digestive systems, their electrical systems, their circulatory systems, and every other system function with 100 percent efficiency.

Jesus Himself bore my children's sicknesses and carried their diseases; therefore, sickness and disease are not allowed to exist in their bodies. Their bodies are free from growths, tumors, or obstructions of any kind.

The divine *zoe* life of God flows through them, quickening and making alive their mortal bodies. My children's bodies are free from pain, discomfort, distress, and all symptoms of sickness. God's Word is medicine to their flesh. I am not moved by how they feel, how they look, or any negative reports, because I believe God's Word and His Word says they are healed. My children are healed, healthy, and whole in Jesus' name.

Scriptures

But he was wounded for our transgressions, he was bruised for our iniquities: the chastisement of our peace was upon him; and with his stripes we are healed.

Isaiah 53:5

My son, attend to my words; incline thine ear unto my sayings. Let them not depart from thine eyes; keep them in the midst of thine heart. For they are life unto those that find them, and health to all their flesh.

Proverbs 4:20-22

He sent his word, and healed them, and delivered them from their destructions.

Psalm 107:20

That it might be fulfilled which was spoken by Esaias the prophet, saying, Himself took our infirmities, and bare our sicknesses.

Matthew 8:17

Who his own self bare our sins in his own body on the tree, that we, being dead to sins, should live unto righteousness: by whose stripes ye were healed.

1 Peter 2:24

My Children Have Pleasant Personalities

I believe my children are kind and considerate of others. They are eager and willing to be a blessing at any opportunity. They have a heart of compassion, and they are easily touched with the hurt and pain of others. They are quick to speak a kind or encouraging word to a friend who is down or discouraged. They are always willing to lend a helping hand to those in need. They are willing to forego their own pleasures in order to be a blessing to others.

They do their chores without complaining and whining. They are ever ready to do their part in working around the house or in the yard.

They are diligent and responsible regarding their school work and other obligations in their lives. They are respectful of their parents and others in positions of authority in their lives. They do not give in to selfish or self-serving desires but are giving and have a servant's heart.

They have pleasant and pleasing personalities. They are gracious and mannerly when interacting with others.

Scriptures

But a certain Samaritian, as he journeyed, came where he was: and when he saw him, he had compassion on him, And went to him, and bound up his wounds, pouring in oil and wine, and set him on his own beast, and brought him to an inn, and took care of him.

Luke 10:33,34

By this shall all men know that ye are my disciples, if ye have love one to another.

John 13:35

A man that hath friends must shew himself friendly: and there is a friend that sticketh closer than a bother.

Proverbs 18:24

And at the end of ten days their countenances appeared fairer and fatter in flesh than all the children which did eat the portion of the king's meat.

Daniel 1:15

My Children's Self-Image

My children have a healthy self-image. They are confident in who they are. They understand that God's love makes them valuable. My children understand that who they are is determined by what God has declared them to be and not by what others say about them. God's Word says that they are precious in His sight. They are children of the Most High God. He has chosen them, and He has great plans for their lives.

My children see themselves as God sees them. They see themselves as more than conquerors through Christ Jesus. They are the head and not the tail, above and not beneath, going over and not under. They see themselves as victorious and triumphant in life.

They are not filled with worry, anxiety, or self-doubt, but courage, boldness, and faith. They realize that they can do all things though Christ, who strengthens them. They think clearly and rationally. My children have a positive attitude and will not allow the circumstances of life to steal their peace.

I declare that my children are confident in their relationship with God, and therefore, they are secure in who they are; they do not give in to thoughts and temptations of insecurity.

Scriptures

Ye are of God, little children, and have overcome them: because greater is he that is in you, than he that is in the world.

1 John 4:4

Nay, in all things we are more than conquerors through him that loved us.

Romans 8:37

Being confident of this very thing, that he which hath begun a good work in you will perform it until the day of Jesus Christ.

Philippians 1:6

I can do all things through Christ which strengtheneth me.

Philippians 4:13

For My Children To Choose Godly Friends

I know it is God's will for my children to have a godly circle of friends. I believe the Holy Spirit will give them discernment regarding the right kind of friends. I believe God will bring my children godly friends who are strong spiritually, who love God, and who will have a positive impact on my children's lives.

I believe the Holy Spirit will lead my children to friends who love God and have a close relationship with Him. The Holy Spirit will help them to be sensitive to the needs of their friends and to encourage them in their spiritual walk. May God be at the center of all their friendships.

I believe my children will develop strong, healthy friendships that will last a lifetime. I believe my children will recognize the true value of close, godly friends. I believe that my children will come to realize that one of God's greatest gifts in this life is the friendship of a true friend.

Scriptures

If any of you lack wisdom, he should ask God, who gives generously to all without finding fault, and it will be given to him.

James 1:5

He that walketh with wise men shall be wise: but a companion of fools shall be destroyed.

Proverbs 13:20

But speaking the truth in love, may grow up into him in all things, which is the head, even Christ: From whom the whole body fitly joined together and compacted by that which every joint supplieth, according to the effectual working in the measure of every part, maketh increase of the body unto the edifying of itself in love.

Ephesians 4:15,16

My Children's Future

God's Word promises me that His covenant blessings are passed down to my children. Therefore, I am in agreement with His Word, and I boldly proclaim that He has prepared a bright and glorious future for my children.

They will live in God's abundance in every area of their lives. God's blessings shall overtake them. They will serve God with gladness and enthusiasm all the days of their lives. My children will honor God by how they conduct their lives. They will be bold witnesses for the kingdom. They have passion and a desire to reach out to hurting people with the good news of the Gospel. They will fulfill all the plans and purposes that God has desired for them to accomplish. God shall direct their steps. They have been trained and nurtured in the Word of God. They will not fall into sin or slide away from God.

God's favor shall be upon them, and they shall succeed at the assignment God has for their lives. My children shall have a spirit of discernment and will not be fooled by people who would try to deceive or discourage them from pursuing God's plan for their lives.

My children will be determined and courageous in their pursuit of all God has for them. They will be quick to take a stand for what is right and against what is wrong. They shall be people of peace and kindness, with a heart of compassion for others. They will endure hardships as good soldiers and face the obstacles and setbacks of life with courage and spiritual resolve.

My children's lives will be a living testimony of God's love, power, and grace. They will live strong, victorious, God-centered lives.

Scriptures

Being confident of this very thing, that he which hath begun a good work in you will perform it until the day of Jesus Christ.
Philippians 1:6

For the gifts and calling of God are without repentance.

Romans 11:29

Therefore, since we have such a hope, we are very bold.

2 Corinthians 3:12

PRAYER OF SALVATION

God loves you—no matter who you are, no matter what your past. God loves you so much that He gave His one and only begotten Son for you. The Bible tells us that "...whosoever believeth in him should not perish, but have everlasting life" (John 3:16). Jesus laid down His life and rose again so that we could spend eternity with Him in heaven and experience His absolute best on earth. If you would like to receive Jesus into your life, say the following prayer out loud and mean it from your heart.

Heavenly Father, I come to You admitting that I am a sinner. Right now, I choose to turn away from sin, and I ask You to cleanse me of all unrighteousness. I believe that Your Son, Jesus, died on the cross to take away my sins. I also believe that He rose again from the dead so that I might be forgiven of my sins and made righteous through faith in Him. I call upon the name of Jesus Christ to be the Savior and Lord of my life. Jesus, I choose to follow You and ask that You fill me with the power of the Holy Spirit. I declare that right now I am a child of God. I am free from sin and full of the righteousness of God. I am saved in Jesus' name. Amen.

If you prayed this prayer to receive Jesus Christ as your Savior for the first time, please contact us on the Web at **www.harrisonhouse.com** to receive a free book.

Or you may write to us at:
Harrison House
P.O. Box 35035
Tulsa, Oklahoma 74153

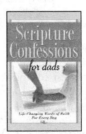